Poems

Written at the Huntington Library

JAMES THORPE

Poems

Written at the Huntington Library

Poems about the Huntington ◎ Poems for Playful People ◎ Poems for Adam and his Successors ◎ Poems for Users of Language ◎ Poems about the Natural World ◎ Poems for Lovers ◎ Poems for Thinkers

JAMES THORPE

THE HUNTINGTON LIBRARY
SAN MARINO, CALIFORNIA

Printed in the United States of America

Cover photograph: Huntington Library
Cover and interior design: Kathleen Thorne-Thomsen

Library of Congress Cataloging-in-Publication Data

Thorpe, James Ernest, 1915–
Poems written at the Huntington Library / James Thorpe.
p. cm.
Contents: Poems about the Huntington—Poems for playful people—Poems for Adam and his successors—Poems for users of language—Poems about the natural world—Poems for lovers—Poems for thinkers.
ISBN: 0-87328-188-8
1. Henry E. Huntington Library and Art Gallery—Poetry. I. Henry E. Huntington Library and Art Gallery. II. Title.

PS3570.H679 P64 2000
811'.54—dc21 00-057229

Huntington Library Press
1151 Oxford Road San Marino CA 91108
www.huntington.org

ACKNOWLEDGMENTS

Several of the poems in the first section, on the Huntington Library, first appeared in the Huntington Calendar *between 1969 and 1983. "In Philosophical Hall" first appeared in the* Proceedings of the American Philosophical Society, *vol. 134, 1990. "Talking With the Birds" first appeared in* Texture *#5, 1993.*

JAMES THORPE *was the Director of the Huntington Library, Art Collections, and Botanical Gardens from 1966 to 1983, and a Senior Research Associate for 1983 to 1999.*

C O N T E N T S

Poems

ABOUT THE HUNTINGTON

In the Japanese Garden
Seven Haiku

Earth and sky embrace
While stones and plants and water
Join in harmony.

Petals drift like snow
Onto our upturned faces
From the bowing plum.

Red maple leans down
Above the pool and we stand
Preserving silence.

Sunlight and rain have
Fallen on his face and still
He meditates in peace.

Men and women walk
On the quiet curving paths
And seem unknown friends.

On a bench, at peace,
Hoping that I can reflect
The tranquil garden.

Overhead the stir
Of leaves, below the sweet sad
Smiling of farewell.

Watching a Covey of Quail in Spring

Through the seasons they have been
Our covey of quail.

We have watched them walk
Erect, alert, nervously intent,
Quick to follow where they're led,
Speaking and answering with a multitude
Of clicks and murmurs that seem
Advice, encouragement, or threat,
Their patterns always changing
Yet always within a network of control.

We have watched them grow
Until their differences are all disposed
Within the bounds of confidence and sex,
Until the mother is
Forgetful of her daughters
And the father of his sons,
Until relations all depend
On guidance through the terrors of the day.

We have watched them scatter
In restless search for generation
Within new bounds of family life.
The timid females forge ahead
Exulting in their seed
And males trail hopefully behind
Until the covey is reborn
In pairs of new identity.

Our need has made them ours
And we have come to think that
Now they belong to us.
We cannot suffer mysteries
Which elude our grasp,
Nor alien conduct
Beyond the bounds of our own doing.

Thus we have made the wild domestic
And the strange is once again
The comfortable familiar,
Their acts converted
Into what we understand
Or can reason into sense.

Coyotes in the Gardens

Like all wild things, the coyotes are
Always alert: they are on constant watch
By nose and ear and eye. One of them sees me
And I stand rigid, hoping to pass for a tree,
But his senses play on me
To find out what I am
And what I plan to do.
At length our contact breaks, by truce,
And each of us turns aside as if
Oblivious to the other.

They are sleek now, like slender German shepherds,
Filled I suppose with tasty mice and rats.
To me they are graceful like dancers,
Poised to move as intuition may suggest,
Instantly ready to turn or stand or slide
Into their next position, always following
Some score for survival, strange,
Aloof, detached, and full of composure.

The young are different.
With less economy of motion
They seem uncertain, and like all young
They have less caution.
Growing up is an exercise in imitation
In which learning to survive comes first
Or all the rest is wasted. But much is lost.

At the wail of a distant siren
Their barks and howls shatter the night
In painful anguish. Their double throats
Multiply the voices rising to object
To this intrusion on their peace.
When this land was wild, it was theirs,
Now they seek to call it back
As the wild mustard reasserts its reign.

Christmas Cookies

(For the Cookie Exchange of the Huntington Volunteers)

Don't ask me
How to make Christmas cookies.
I've never made any
Though I've eaten a lot of good ones
And some not so good perhaps
But I enjoyed them anyway.

So I speak to you
Strictly as a consumer of Christmas cookies
And not as a producer of them
(As many of you are)
Nor as an administrator of the kitchen
And certainly not as a cookie-executive
But just as a fair-minded consumer of cookies
And I have these general comments to make
In the place of a regular recipe.

It's my impression
That cookies have to be made
With affection
Just as everything does
If it's going to amount to anything.
I notice that you follow this principle

In what I am privileged
To see of your activities in general
And so I take the liberty
Of inferring what your practice is
In the making of Christmas cookies.

So before you preheat your oven
To three hundred and fifty degrees
Or take down your flour container
And your sugar and spices
And get your butter and milk and eggs
Out of the refrigerator
And line up your cookie cutters
And your bowls and pans and baking sheets
And get ready to go to work
Let me try to put into words
What it is that you do first.

You think a little about the people
Who are going to eat the cookies
Children or friends or grandchildren
Or whoever it's going to be
Maybe we don't even know

Who they will be
And that doesn't matter.
Anyway, you somehow put into those cookies
The most important ingredient of all
Your affection for people.

And it's mainly because of that ingredient
That the cookies are so important
When we give them to one another
And exchange them back and forth
And take them as a sign
That we truly wish for each other
And for all the world
A joyous, loving Christmas time.

Feathers

Feathers are precious gifts
they appear unsought
but you have to be
on the lookout for them
they are all different like people
and all precious
if you like feathers or people
and can tolerate mystery
without asking too many
unanswerable questions like
why did it come to me or
what does this one mean or
where will it lead me
well the truth is we don't know
why these gifts come to us
or what lets us find them
or pass them up
we do know that
nothing is lost in giving ever
or almost never
usually there's a gain
in letting go and giving up

a feather.

The World as an Enclosure of Trees

This is our place,
Together, here under these trees.

Shady, surrounded by shrubs,
Kaleidoscopic sky, grassy floor,
Folding us within its leafy arms.

The jays sweep in and land squawking
While squirrels chatter overhead
And chase about the sequoias.
The quail walk sagely by
And murmur their content.

The outside world mirrors the world within.
This world accepts our presence
As we accept ourselves
For we are part of it
And it is part of us.

This is our place,
Together, here under these trees.
It is the world
In which we belong
To each other.

Among the Camellias

This is the third time
We have seen the camellias
Begin to grow.

After sasanquas, the glory of japonicas:
Pink Perfection is among the first,
Then pouting Tinsie and pointed Fircone,
And a stunning multitude of others.

But we have looked
Not so much as plant people
But rather as lovers of beauty,
As lovers of the world outside the self.
As for me, I felt that I was being guided
By some mysterious force
To share perceptions with another
And come together thus in joy.

Not by these views alone, of course,
But of many other things, like quail
And coyotes, Shakespeare
And Wallace Stevens, children
And other friends, as well as the living truths
Of what we are and what we mean to be.

The blooming season for camellias is now
Drawing to its annual close.
This is only the third time we have seen them
Begin to grow.

In the Desert Garden

The world is filled with mystery
And strange sights appear on every side.
Yucca and euphorbia
Puyas and agave and golden barrel cacti--
All are alien to eyes
That have been trained on oaks and pines.
So too are mammillaria and crassula
Instead of myrtle, holly, and nandina.

We bring the strange into our lives
By likening it to what we think we know.
We call these plants a crown of thorns or a pincushion,
Cow's horns or an elephant's foot
Or a prickly pear. The names we give them
Tell of our own sense of their forbidding nature.
To them we join the band of predators
That they have learned to outwit
With thorny spines and hard surfaces,
With acrid juices and disguise, in the course of
Eras of survival against the ancient threats
Of ancestors of the rat and lizard,
Burro and peccary and the ground sloth.

The world outside threatens an unprotected life.
These desert plants have taught themselves
To fight the fierceness of the sun
And lack of rain by hiding their reserves
In swollen leaves and stems. Many have lost
The struggle and have disappeared
From every range of memory.

The will to live is the force
That makes these forms and shapes,
And the struggle to survive has left
T hese contortions as the markers of success:
Strange sights, filled with mystery.

Trumpet Vines

The tendrils of these vines
Wrap them together
In spiral convolutions,
Enveloping one another.
From their rich planting bed of woods earth
They rise and ascend this arbor.

Many vines were planted here,
But most of them have perished
Or else keep up a bare pretense of life.
Only these two remain in luxurious health,
And they have now converged
High on this arbor, in a spot
Favored by broken sun at midday
And by shadows in the afternoon,
Leaving large gaps of empty trelliswork
Ugly and bare against the sky.

Years ago I should have taken out
The weaker plants, perhaps, to give light and air
To those that promised better growth.

Now it is very hard to trace the stems
Back to their roots. In many ways it is impossible
To separate the living from the dead, particularly
Since death comes so subtly and in
So many different forms
While the stems are still transmitting vital force.
Likewise, in such a tangle pruning is a dangerous task
And painful when a stem, cut at the ground
Turns out to be the one alive
With leaves and flowers out toward the end.

I think with longing of this arbor
As it might have been,
If I had thinned and pruned these vines
When they were rank in growth
And apt for training.
Thick and lush and full of flowers,
There would have been no bareness
Near their beginnings
And none of those naked spots
To spoil the pattern of their beauty.

But these are backward thoughts
Rising to depose the present.
There is still time to prune these vines,
Release them from restraint
And give them a chance to flourish.
Perhaps they will not;
Perhaps the arbor cannot be improved
Except in dreams.
I do not know the answers.
But these are the questions of moment because
The question is always now.

Saturday Is Just Like Any Other Day of the Week Except Better

The world talks to you
and tells you its secrets.
The squirrel chattering overhead
is explaining the troubles he has to face,
and the distant quail is calling
to express his need for a mate.
The deodar cedars beam their fragrance
down on you in the warm sun,
and the tips of a sequoia branch
pluck at your hair as you pass,
telling you what they are like.
The woodpecker that lands on the tree beside you
is intent on his constant search for food
while a coyote walks quietly
beyond the thin shrubs that give
comfort to his need for privacy.
We listen to the things the world is saying

and find that they are not so much secrets
after all but rather the open truths
of the world in which we live
and of ourselves
          mainly ourselves
                    mostly our selves.

Meeting And Greeting And Saying Goodbye

We walk among the deodars
And smell the pungent fragrance
That the sun draws out of their needles,
Filling the area with a sense
Of the presence of these trees.
Then around by the camellias
Radiant with white and pink and red
At this season of the year,
Sending out their signals of what
Is going on within them and
Inviting us to respond if we know how.
And up through the rose garden
With its stand-offish dress of thorns
And prickly stems on guard to warn away
Hungry predators and others who might want
To intrude into their private winter space.
The world is full of signs and symbols
That can open up the mysteries around us
If we know how to notice them
And see what they are meant to mean.

Whenever we venture outside the circle of the self
We too display a store of signs that say things
Like welcome or let's try or think carefully
Or take care or go away please,
And from there our messages go deep and deeper.
The most important things are unspoken, as in
Meeting and greeting and saying goodbye.

Poems

for Playful People

The Charge of the Light Brigade

The summer sun is going down—
Mosquitoes, take your posts!
It is the time for us to be
Satan's avenging hosts.
All good deeds in this naughty world
We'll pay back with a will
With buzzes, bites, and scratching whelps
Till we have had our fill.
So see that your probosces are
Sharp and clean and ready.
Test your wings and start your whine
Until you have it steady.
You common culex, form the front
Of our attacking band--
The others join at either flank
To sweep across the land.
Go for the handsome women first
For their good deeds are great;
Besides their arms and legs are out
Susceptible to fate.
Avoid the men until the end

For they're not worth the trouble;
They do no deeds of any note
And their hide's full of stubble.
Our cause is just, our hearts are pure
In all our buzzing band.
The sun has sunk, the stars are out
And supper is at hand.

How To Tell Tother From Which

"He can't tell tother from which." (colloquial, late 19th–20th century)

Everyone knows which which is bewitched
And when you must tether a tother,
But I will reveal the secrets of how
To distinguish the one from the other.
Tother is the one with the big bay boon
While which has a scratch on his pod;
He makes a point of not coughing out loud
And the other one rarely goes shod.
If you will remember to stand on your toes
And look at the whites of their eyes
You'll notice that tother's unusually round
While which has a look of surprise.
This way you can easily stay out of school
And still be exceedingly wise.

Talking With The Birds

Hello there, jay bird!
What are you up to,
Making all that racket on our roof?
You sound like a student burglar
Trying to learn how to break in.
Oh, I see, you're working on one of our acorns.
Well, that's better than swooping around
And squawking and chasing all the shyer birds away.
Why are you so loud and bossy?
You don't have so much to be proud of
Except your appearance. I do admit
That your colors are worth looking at,
But everybody knows that your beauty is only
Feather-deep. What counts is
What use you make of your talents and attributes,
And I'm very much afraid that
You are just a show-off.
Are you trying to compensate for
Some deep insecurity with all that brassiness?
I would be glad to help you
If you would like to talk it over with me.
Generally you just put an end to our discourse
By flying away.

The jay bird replies:

Well, I tend to fly away
Because you people seem to find it impossible
To carry on any intelligent discourse
With anybody except yourselves,
And I'm not even sure about your private talk.
I'll break my rule
And try to explain it to you,
But I doubt that you'll understand
Any more than you have in the past.
Your fundamental problem is that
You look on the world as a very large supermarket
Of which you are both the owner and the only customer.
For millenia you believed in a myth of the world
As a Great Chain of Being
With you up there at the top right below the Creator
And everything else somewhere down below you
Doing its little bit to keep your chain complete.
Some of you are beginning to grumble that
Many of your own kind are given to racism
And homophobia and anti-feminism
And a dozen other forms of discrimination and ignorance.
How about all of you as a class?

"Genericists" we would call you
If we had your sense of superiority over all other
kinds of creatures.
But it turns out better for us
Just to fly away.

(Translated from the Avian by James Thorpe)

Tit for Tat

Tat is for tit
And tit is for tat

I'll try to sit
Just where you sat

You eat a bit
And I'll go to bat

I hope for a hit
But you wear the hat

You can be fit
But I will get fat

I'll have the pit
And give you a pat

You take the chit
And I will go chat

I'll chase the nit
And you swat the gnat

You bring the kit
And I'll pet the kat

Tat is for tit
And tit is for tat

Biting the Bullet and Eating the Crow

This crow got shot in flapping flight
While cawing at a friend;
You too have made a grave mistake
And now's the time to mend.
So you must bite the bullet first
That took the dark bird's life,
Then masticate the crow itself
Without a fork or knife.
Now here's the bullet that got the crow
The one just right for you,
Munch it lightly and bite it hard
And have a nutritious chew.
Then take a piece of this fine bird,
A drumstick or a wing,
Enjoy the flavor of his meat
And let the welkin ring!
So here's to the ones who make mistakes
Like the crow and you and me—
Some get shot and some get eaten
But we lucky ones go free.

Getting Together

Bonny lass, pretty lass, wilt thou be mine?
Thou shalt not wash dishes,
Nor yet serve the swine;
Thou shalt sit on a cushion, and sew a fine seam,
And thou shalt eat strawberries, sugar, and cream!

—Mother Goose

Bright friend, able friend, may we unite?
Both at home and at work
We will have much delight;
Our thoughts will be subject to inter-review,
And we'll share the decisions in all that we do!

—Father Gander

Getting a Word in Edgewise

If you can't get a word in edgewise,
Please consider the words that you try.
Are you offering terms like <u>inspissate</u>
In the hope of a <u>synergy</u> high?
<u>Stercoricolous</u> palls on the nostrils
Nor will <u>syzygy</u> light up the sky.

These words are all too wide and thick
To slide into the crack
That's left when talkers pause for breath
While driving down their track.

What you need is a store of edgewise words
That are smooth and slick and crafty,
That will open up some windows
And will make the discourse drafty.

If you think that sex will do the trick
You're sadly out of date,
For it's money-making words that count
When you pontificate.

Speak options and commodities,
  Securities at risk,
Suggest the Mae girls, Fan and Gin,
  When bid and asked are brisk.

Think yield to maturity and P/E multiple,
  Go long with every shelter.
Your T-Bills, futures, tax-exempts
  Can come out helter skelter.

These edgewise words will earn your place
  In almost any state,
Provided you don't lose your nerve
  And rehypothecate.

Wrestling with a Strong Verb

We wrestled there
All through the night
        I strive, he strove, we have striven
All through the night
        He strikes, I struck
        I drive, he drove
        He throws, I threw
        I catch, he caught
        He dives, I dove
        I give, he gave
        He stinks, I stank
        I fall, he fell
        He holds, I held
Let me go, he said
For the day is breaking
        It breaks, it broke, it has broken
I will not let you go
Unless you bless me
        I hide, I hid, I am hidden
What is your name, he said
Or how do you call yourself?

He knows, he knew, he has known
What is your name, I said
Or what shall I call you?
I rise, I rose, I have risen
Why do you ask my name, he said?
He speaks, he spoke, he has spoken
And he blessed me there
He sings, I sang, we have sung
Together.

In Praise of Peccadilloes

The world is full of likelihood
For doing something wrong,
For falling into errancy
Amongst transgression's throng.

Please talk not of the deadly sins
And other falls from grace
For peccadilloes are the most
That I know how to face.

Dear peccadillo, my close friend,
I hold you in my arms
To keep away those wicked faults
That cause so many harms.

Oh I'm peccable and peccant
In my peccability
And when peccancy defeats me
There's a possibility
That a peccadillo will survive
And help to set me free.

Tom, Dick, and Harry

"And don't waste a lot of time . . . staying away from advantageous parties to eat in little cafes down-town with Tom, Dick, and Harry."
(Mrs. Connage in F. Scott Fitzgerald's "This Side of Paradise," 1920)

It's true that I'm not very bright,
Said Harry with a sigh.
Well, on the social scale, said Tom,
I never rated high.
I fear, said Dick, that I am just
An ordinary guy.

While Morgan, Miles, and Amory
Were made of other clay,
And Dexter, Dwight, and Percival
Are people to obey.
Let Stafford, Seth, and Ferdinand
Combine to save the day.

With Chauncey, Clark, and Algernon,
The dining's more than food,
And Geoffrey, Glenn, and Meredith
Would never dare be rude,
While Herschel, Hugh, and Frederick—
Another magnitude!

Since Ernest, Earl, and Roderick
Display a stylish frown,
And Dunstan, Dale, and Oliver
Deserve to wear a crown,
So Lowell, Lyle, and Cameron
Would never go down-town.

Well, let's go out and have a bite
Said Tom, who felt quite free
While Dick and Harry added that
They'd heartily agree:
We'll go down-town and join some folks
Without a pedigree.

Ubi Sunt?

Where are they now?
Those usual childhood diseases
Of measles and mumps
And being kept in bed
With wintry sniffles?
Those games presided over
By kindly parents of the birthday child
Of Going to Jerusalem
And Blindman's Buff?
Those awkward times
While being taught to dance
Of having to seek a partner
Or be sought?
Those embarrassed silences
That followed after being called on
Until one had to admit
To not being prepared?
Those long, long waits
Before being chosen
When sides were being
Picked for games?

Where are they now?
They are alive and well
And practising on
Yet another generation of children
To prepare them for the rigors
Of adolescence.

Old Saws And Ancient Wood

I wanted to try to make
A silk purse out of a sow's ear
So that I would no longer have to live
From hand to mouth and
By hook or by crook and
Between the devil and the deep blue sea.

But there were problems
And it kept raining cats and dogs
Between the rock and the hard place
Where I lived. But then
A child came up to me and said
"Why don't you give this up
And just make a mountain out of a mole hill?"

I thought this was a fair to middling idea
To come out of the mouths
Of babes and sucklings
So I went looking for mole hills
Up hill and down dale
Across the river and into the trees.

But no mole hills or sow's ears
Could I find, from China to Peru
So I concluded that a bird in the hand
Was worth two in the bush
And that I might as well
Go ahead and rob Peter to pay Paul
And go to hell in a handbasket.

Poems

FOR ADAM AND HIS SUCCESSORS

Why it was that Adam, not God, Named the Creatures

God is a wise executive
as we ought to know
and so he delegated to Adam
the extensive task
of naming all the creatures
great and small
every single last beast of the field
and fowl of the air.
Business School people say that it was
to get Adam involved
as near the beginning as he was
around for
and thus give him a share in the grave
responsibility.
Psychologists say that it was explicitly
a test of Adam to see
how he would handle the task
but actually a test

of God's unresolved self seen in the

powers passed on to Adam.

Feminists say that it was intended as a slap

in the face of Eve

to have the naming done before

she was created

thus proving once again that

God is male.

I say that God had already done

a good week's work

and he didn't want to spoil

his day off

by having to attend to any

more details.

Adam's First Lesson In The Use Of Language

I

When God brought the beasts of the field
Before Adam to see what he would call them,
Adam was full of pep and imagination.
"Giraffe" and "elephant" fell easily from his lips,
As did "rhinoceros" and "kangaroo".
He slyly called out "hippopotamus"
So that the Greeks could have a river horse
After they had developed words of their own.

II

But when God started the fly by
Of the fowls of the air, Adam's inventiveness
Began to flag.
Soon he had to resort to double names
To describe them and give them their identity.
At first he gave out names
That told how he saw or heard the birds,
Like "bald eagle" and "screech owl" and "scrub jay",
Then "solitary sandpiper" and "white-bellied booby"

With an occasional burst of prevision like "prothonotary warbler".
But pretty soon he was satisfied with things like
"Lesser Canada goose" and "lesser nighthawk",
And then with "least flycatcher" and "least petrel"
And finally with such as "common cowbird" and "common crow"
And "common egret" and "common bushtit".

III

After a while, God got a little restless
With the ordinariness of the names that Adam was giving
To the birds that God had been so particular to create.
"Don't you realize," He said to Adam, "that every creature
Is full of meaning and should have a name
That points to the essence of its being
And not how you perceive it from without?
Also, you're messing up the sense
That these creatures will have of themselves
By leading them to believe that they are at bottom

'Lesser' or 'common',
Or that 'bald' or 'white-bellied'
Is the center of their selves.
So be careful. I made language
Before I created you. And you had better learn
To be as respectful of our words
As of our creatures
And how you treat them all."

Speaking Your Name

And out of the ground the Lord God formed every beast of the field, and every fowl of the air; and brought them unto Adam to see what he would call them: and whatsoever Adam called every living creature, that was the name thereof. And Adam gave names to all cattle, and to the fowl of the air, and to every beast of the field.

Genesis 2. 19–20

I

I look at you, said Adam,
And I know instantly
What makes you real
And therefore what your name is.
You have an essence within you,
An essence with which the Lord God
Endowed you and made it yours.
I just stand there and receive
The radiations that emanate from you.
They put themselves into words,
And that is what you are
To be called.
All I have to do is
Speak your name.
Thus have I been given the privilege
Of making you real for mankind.

II

The time will come
When things will not be so clear,
When the radiations will be obscured
And the senses will no longer possess
Much of their original power of knowing.
Then there will have to be much talk
About signs and symbols and emblems,
About allegory and myth and metaphor
And all sorts of other figures
That may be resorted to as ways
Of trying to understand
What cannot be readily known
And of penetrating the burden
Of what will be called the mystery.
Enough at least to get some sense
Of what it is that lies out there
Beyond our ever diminishing power
To understand and be understood.
Then it will not be enough
Just to speak your name.

III

But the power will still remain
To know and to be known
By being responsive to the radiations
That will continue to emanate
From that inner essence
That is unquenchable so long
As there is life.
Thus we will always be able, if we choose,
To share our deepest identity with one another.
A man will be able to know a woman
And a woman know a man
By seeking out that inner radiance
And responding to it with your own.
People will come to call this love,
And I like that way
Of talking about it.
But it is still what I meant
In the beginning when I talked of
Speaking your name.
It is how I felt
About the beasts of the field
And the fowl of the air
And all creation.

Talking It Over With God

When I was little
I was mighty impressed
By all the stories about you
In those early books of the Bible.
You were certainly tops in creativity
As well as in power and anger.
And then in those later books
You showed another side of yourself
Through all those stories about Jesus and love
And how to get along with one another.
Later I heard it said
That these were all just myths,
Folk tales written down a long time after the supposed event.
But other people argued that you had in fact
Dictated the whole thing yourself, word for word.
I was puzzled for a while until I began to realize
That probably it doesn't much matter which way it was,
That myth can be just as good at conveying
Truth or falsehood as the accounts by participants.
Sometimes better, or sometimes even the only way.
Also, I really don't understand deep truths
Except in human terms. I have to hear
About people sowing seeds and reaping the harvest,
Or what happens to ill-dressed guests at a wedding feast,

Or about those with lamps that do and do not work,
Or how different people handle large sums of money they
receive.
And this reminds me of another thing:
About what people call the Nature of Reality.
This question has probably been kicked around
Ever since you let people begin to think.
But it's only a little while ago
That most people have stopped kicking stones
To show what's real and have instead
Begun to construct elaborate theories
(As literary scholars are adept at doing)
To show that no one can understand anything
With any kind of accuracy,
Or that it can be known only in the terms
That my theory makes possible.

After bringing God up to date on all these things,
I stopped to see what kind of answer he would make.
I guess that he agreed with what I'd said,
Because he just gave me an affectionate look
And smiled.

Poems

for Users of Language

Dreaming of Christmas

A Dialogue between Santa Claus and Me

Me.   Dear Santa, please leave in my stocking
A package of very straight words
to cut through
the utterances of pundits
the eloquence of sellers
the promises of public men.

Santa. Are you sure that's what you want?
Those words might turn out
to leave your discourse
curling at the edges
drying on the surface
losing its pigmentation.

Me.   I thought that language was the place
To make a start if we want
to give up
contriving effects
creating illusions
manipulating people.

Santa. No, language is the place you end
If you are moving in that direction
you start by
whistling at reindeers
twinkling your eyes
dreaming of Christmas.

Conversion

Memory is the act
By which we change
Sensation into truth.

All pains and pleasures are
Tentative until
We validate them with
The stamp and seal of remembering
And thus put them into order.

No one is complex enough
To see at once
The meaning of his dreams
When they unfold before him
And become his life.
The best that we can do is
To record the events
Of those rare moments
And let memory give them
Passage through our selves
To fill the empty spaces
Of our lives with richness.

Thus speak I,
A modern Moses,
A self-appointed perceiver
Of the unseen currents
In human life.
Whether these things
Are true for you
I do not know.
But I must tell them
This way because
I wish to celebrate the joy
That I now know.

Advice on the Use of the Apostrophe

(a short fit induc'd by looking at the Chicago Manual of Style)

Don't look for Xerxes' army
In Jefferson Davis's homes
Nor seek for Marx's theories
In any of Dickens's tomes.
James Gibbs's London churches
Euripides' play
The skull and crossbones' meaning
All have Margaux's bouquet.
The Joneses' reputation
And the Williamses' land
With all of Burns's poems
For conscience' sake must stand.
Since Moses' leadership
Passed on in Jesus' name
In three days' time contributes
To Demosthenes' fame.
  Wie geht's? was gibt's?
  Hab' ich Leibniz?
  Quel l'uomo de'
  Malevoli!

Elegy on the Loss of a Favorite Word

I had always been fond
of the word nubile.
It brought to my mind
an attractive young woman
gifted, charming, bright
with beauty of body and spirit
and lithe in her responses
to the impingements of the outer world.
But alas I have come to realize
that I have loaded this word
with my own vision
that doesn't necessarily match
its sense of simply being
old enough for marriage.
So here is a word
that has to be retired from this use
and gratefully pensioned with thanks
for all those services rendered.
But only the word.
The vision
remains.

Retirement Ceremony for the Word WONDERFUL

I

Please step forward,
Wonderful.
Accept our heartfelt thanks

For serving well
And faithfully
By filling in the blanks.

You've done the job
When our dim wit
Was muddled or austere

You've saved us from
Aphasia
Throughout your long career.

No longer need
You be on call
To help participate:

You're free to travel
When you like--
Retirements liberate.

II

Each of us
Who's left behind
Will have to scratch his head

And come upon
Some other words
To conjure with instead.

We'll get good help
From Fine and Choice,
And Super, Splendid, Glorious,

Fussy First-Rate
Will do his share,
And so will kindly Marvelous.

Superior,
Outstanding, and
Old standby Excellent,

Select, Deluxe,
Superb, Supreme,
And sound Beneficent,

Unparalleled,
Preeminent
Can jump into the breach.

But Wonderful,
Dear Wonderful,
Please teach them all your speech.

Watching the Sky

What do you mean
"I don't understand it."
Who does? Some teacher
Must have told you
That you should try
To understand everything.
What is the meaning of
The pattern of those two
Sequoias against the evening sky?
Or the sound of that dog
Barking in the neighbor's yard
While they are away.
Or the smell of the soil
That was watered yesterday.
Go to it if you want to
Become a renowned expert.
Tell us what it all means.
It's easy--
All you need is a control of language
And the knack of making new terms
Or of adapting old ones

To an unexpected use.
Perhaps we will revere you
As an expert,
As a great scholar,
As a perceptive, learned,
Penetrating personage.
Or perhaps not.
If we are cranky enough
We will see that you
Are talking about
What we must all understand
Quietly in the spirit
But not necessarily
Noisily in the mouth.

Poems

ABOUT THE NATURAL WORLD

The Other

How can we learn to share
In the life outside our selves?
There's a lot going on
Out there, all sorts of things.
The birds are busy with their tasks,
The clouds keep changing their clothes,
And the trees must seem to the stones
To be growing at a mad pace.
And people! You can hardly ever tell
What's up with them, or even whether
They know themselves.
So how to share in all this action?
By that much commended
Wise passiveness which makes the world
Come knocking on your door?
By being quiet and trying to appreciate
Some part of what is happening
All around us?
By becoming actively involved
In the deep purpose of things
Outside ourselves?

And if you think any of these work,
Then how in the dickens do you do it?
Of course you can avoid the whole question
Simply by saying that everything
Outside ourselves is a mystery
That cannot be understood
And that it is improper to
Intrude into it.
And yet if we want to be alive
We have to give our own cellular organization
The chance to grow a little.
We can at least make a start
By seeing that there is something else
Out there of value,
Like birds or sky or trees or people.
And that maybe we can learn
To understand them better
For what they really are
And perhaps even
Learn to love them.

Beach Thoughts

What is there to see?
That man walking upon the beach
With the bottoms of his trousers rolled
Listening to the surge of the wide, wide sea
That chafes on the unnumbered idle pebbles
Watching the spume that plays
Upon a ghostly paradigm of things
And observing that earth has not
Anything to show more fair
After a form of fire
Approaches the cretonnes of his senses.
Yes, there is all that to see
All that and more, much more
Of what our masters have seen before us
Everything or nothing, perhaps, remembered passion,
Unless soul clap its hands and sing.

Tide Pools

The gulls keep watch
From the highest rocks
Heads into the wind
Unperturbed as I clamber out
And move on wary footing
Testing the balance of each rock
Seeking a way to reach the pools
Left by the receding tide
Within a random design of rocks
Thrown there by the giant hand of the sea
As if it had been impatient
To finish this task and move along
To something worth its attention.

They say that life
Began in the sea
And I am drawn by mindless desire
Back to that origin of being
Here at this rocky pool
That the sea feeds
Now with swirling, foaming generosity

And now sucking its gifts away
Until only this sandy universe remains
Preserving in hidden equilibrium
Habitat for a handful of tiny creatures
That take the place of those
From which we all began.

Secrets are revealed
To those who try to see
But in this pool there seems to be
Nothing but easy flowing water
With sea weed swaying to its melody
And light refracted through its shifting prism
Onto the sand and rocks
Until the sand begins to move
As one shell emerging crawls away
And another world takes shape
When motionless creatures quicken
And readjust themselves to the sea
From which we all began.

Going Back To School

We are taught
To consider everything
Intellectually.
How many birds are there
On the patio this evening?
What is the proportion
Of sparrows, cowbirds,
Mourning doves, and brown towhees?
How does that compare
With yesterday
Or with last year?
Why are the sparrows
The only ones that keep on feeding their young
After they are big enough
To look after themselves?
Why are the cowbirds always
Pointing their heads up to the sky?
Why are the mourning doves the only ones
Always wanting to copulate?
Why are the brown towhees
So stand-offish and reclusive?
These are congenial questions:

Even if we don't know how to respond,
They are doubtless answerable
Through study or research.
But how about considering
The beauty of the birds
Or our own deepest feelings
As we look out at this scene
Or muse on what is happening
Inside of us.
These things too
We try to intellectualize,
Usually with some kind of jargon words
That we have been given to understand
Are tools that will
Open up the truth.
It is easy enough to respond
To the world outside
If we are comfortable with ourselves.
Sometimes feeling is desperately easy to do
But almost impossible to explain.
Still, feeling is the heart
Of our existence.

The World As Affirmation

Falling petals

from a flowering plum

Strawflowers

and the first rose

Bay leaves

from the mountains

Cymbidiums

in abundance

Feathers

and cactus flowers

Red-tailed hawk

on the back of a bench

A baby quail

and three coyote cubs

The world's bounty

freely given

like love

Christmas At Laguna Beach, 1981

Birds keep no calendar
Of saints' days or festivals,
No daily reminder of engagements
And of events not to forget.

Sandpipers scurry on the beach
Staying ahead of the surging surf,
Pausing at its momentary turn
To poke their bills into the wet sand.
A squadron of brown pelicans
Sails in close formation near the water
Almost touching it with their wing tips.
The gulls stand their ground
Unruffled by the wind
Making the minimum adjustment
To any intrusion on their lives.

We have left our calendars behind
And walk barefooted on the beach
Dabbling in the surf
Looking for shells and pebbles
That delight the hand and eye
While they are wet with the colors of the sea.

A migratory whale moves slowly toward the south
Rising and spouting in his undulating course.
Sea lions bob their heads up
In the calm beyond the breakers,
And a diving duck practises his trade.
Snorkelers bring in an octopus
That writhes and changes color on the beach
Becoming tan and brown.
The sunset spreads from a concentrate of red
To orange and salmon and pastel pink
Plastered over the western sky,
Changing every minute
Against a background of clear blue
With the evening star hung in place.

This is the world of consciousness
That occupies the body.
Beneath these sensations are the deep echoes
Of Christmases past, and the feelings
That make those memories real.
Feelings for loved ones,
Wherever they are,
At Christmas and all the year.

From the Inside Looking Out and In

I can see the mountains from the window
If I crane a little toward the north.
But from the bed the view is of the tops
Of flat warehouses spreading to the east of the hospital
Across Fair Oaks and Raymond and Arroyo.
Both are good to look at. The one majestic,
The other on a quiet human scale.
I am content to be where I am and who I am,
In the presence of what is set before me:
The roofs meet one another at different levels
And slide away together in patterns
Which submerge the intricacy of their differences
Into the simplicity of apparent regularity.
The rows of ventilators form diagonals
Racing into some other land. The intermittent
Puffs of steam hide a part in shifting uncertainty
And then reveal it as different
From the way it was before.
The rising heat makes patches of distortion,
And the view is full of life and change.
I do not know why we seem to value
The works of nature above the works of man.

Poems

for Lovers

The First Coming

Season of mystery, season of doubt.

If we had been this way before,
We might be able to predict
Where this uncertain journey
Would lead us.

Experience is our comfort,
And out of facts we can
Infer, conclude, and plan
A network of endeavor
Leading to peace of mind.

As it is, we must depend
On prophecy, the croaking voice
That mingles hopes and fears
And deepens what we were before.

Shall we turn back
And validate the past,
Or shall we push ahead
Into a land where we feel
Ill prepared to choose our guide?

Season of mystery, season of doubt.

Gift of the Self

An Old-Fashioned Song

I bring you this handful of pebbles
Rolled smooth by the wrath of the sea:
This one was gold when I found it
And this, purple by royal decree;
Each of them gleamed iridescent
Jewels for giving, from me.

But now when I hand you my present
The pebbles are drab, browns and grays
I pause at their lack of distinction
And wish I could call back their rays.

But you will remember their colors
With a mind that is loving and free
And you will endow them with glory
To match their own native degree.
So I bring you this handful of pebbles
Rolled smooth by the wrath of the sea.

Explicit

That is to say:
  I wish I were with you
This is to say:
  Your heart is my goal
That is to say:
  I live when I see you
This is to say:
  Your love makes me whole.

Song

I see you everywhere
At the focus of my view.

I feel your presence
In the midst of all I do.

I find that everyone
Keeps dissolving into you.

Remembrance of Time Present

I have no words
That are deep enough
To tell about my sense
Of what it means
To be together
Close, close, close, beyond all imagining
Close to one another
Within the world of nature
And yet beyond its bounds.

I can only say:
 It is the essence
   Of living
 And the epitome
   Of love.

First Love

A Song for One or Two Voices

Female voice	How can I tell Whether you love me? How can I dare Think that you do?
Male voice	All of my life I have been cautious Why should I risk Danger with you?
Female voice	All that you say Fills me with wonder, Magical words Vibrantly new.
Male voice	All that I feel Thrills me in sharing Thoughts of a life Bound up with you.
Together	How can I tell Whether you love me? Now I can dare Know that you do.

The Day the World Was Changed

Day of joy, day of comfort.
You came into the world
And the world was changed
For me. I didn't know it
Then but I have known it
Now for a long time
And I will know it yes
Forever. So I rejoice
Today and every day
And keep a holiday
In my heart.

The Continental Divide

The world disappears before me
As my thoughts turn to you,
The continent that's between us
Is divided into two;
The worries that surround me
Become as vague as dew.

When my eyes turn to the mountains
In the distance of the view,
I can see your face before me
No matter what I do,
And I'm sure my love is waiting
In a world that's always new.

As the sunset turns to evening
And the shadows first come through,
My soul is dragged before me
In its yearning after you;
I seek only for the union
Of one continent out of two.

What They Call Love Is Hard to Pin Down in Any One Place

Love is quiet, watchful,
Waiting to creep in
And fill some need.

Love is bold, possessive,
Eager to spend its force
On any fragile thing.

Love is friendly, kind,
Charged with longing for
The chance to show compassion.

Love is sly, cunning,
Full of eyes that see
Itself in others.

Love is easy, soft,
Tolerant toward those who wish
To sit apart.

Love is perceptive, acute,
Quick to chill from
A breath of coldness.

Love is silly, gay,
Pregnant with cheerfulness,
Eager to please.

Love is gentle, willing,
Glad to respond
To firmness and to trust.

Love is shy, retiring,
Afraid to come forward
And risk a rebuff.

Love is grave, sincere,
Preoccupied with the importance
Of being itself.

Three Ways of Trying to Come to Terms with Separation, Perhaps

Separation is a trial form of death, perhaps,
An exercise for the spirit
In preparation for we don't know what
But what we think will sometime be forever,
When what we call our selves will be
Beyond the knowing of the very wise.

Separation is a trial form of independence, perhaps,
An exercise for the spirit
In trying to learn how to deal with
That first aloneness which wants to keep
At least one central part private
And solitary even in the midst of friends.

Separation is a trial form of union, perhaps,
An exercise for the spirit
In building up and testing out the linkages
Through which we may learn how
To guide ourselves and feel
No matter where we are we are together.

The Advantages Of Being Apart Are Relatively Minor

When I turn to you
    I create
The images of your smile

When I think of you
    I release
The sources of inner joy

When I dream of you
    I become
The self I would like to be.

Morning Song

You walked out of my life
Last night
And I didn't cry

You took all of my joy
All right
And I wondered why

I had nothing to say
At all
For my mouth was dead

I had nothing to feel
The fall
When my heart had fled

Let me beg you to bring
The part
That you took away

Let me tell you that you
Can start
All that I call day

In Returning Is Our Peace

Notes for an Unwritten Poem

I looked for you
In every face I saw

I felt the emptiness
Of populated rooms

I kept returning
To awareness of your love

Fitful and restless
I slept with broken dreams

In darkness I awoke
And made a truce with hope.

Yesterday, Today, and Tomorrow

I look at you
And you are always beautiful.
Your deep eyes are rich
With contemplation,
But their seriousness is edged
With a sense of fun.
Reserve stands guard
Over affection's friendly ways
And an undertone of mystery
Shadows the open front.
I come to know you for who you are
And to admire you
More and more
With every measure of passing time.
I look at you
And you are always more beautiful.

There Is More Than One Selfish Way Of Looking At Love

You give
And you take away

You give
    visions of another world without in which
    a kaleidoscope of changing shapes and colors
    turns to a bursting sunrise

And you take away
    turmoil from another world within and make
    a storm of driving winds and snow
    subside into a peaceful landscape

You take away
And you give.

The Release

When you nudged me gently
And asked for room,
I was at first surprised.
I had thought that my heart
Had space enough
Only for me.

But I wriggled a little
And squeezed aside,
Feeling self righteous
In agreeing to share
A corner that already was
Fully in use.

In the beginning it was
A pretty tight fit,
And I breathed carefully
When I began wanting to make
Room for you.

Then I wished I could be
Smaller, so that you'd feel
Comfortable there
Where you had taken
The trouble to be.

But I was astonished to find
That I was growing larger instead
And that, even so,
There was room to move about
As I had never
Done before.

And so it has been,
Increasingly.

But it was a long time
Before I realized that it was you
Who had made all the effort
And taken the risks
Of coming out of your self,
In order to free
The creature within my heart.

Notes for Guidance through Dark Places

I have thought about death
Not often
But enough to keep in mind
The tangible benefits of the gift of life

I have thought about solitude
A little
And have come to feel that it is
A temporary pleasure in the world of man

I have thought about parting
In terror
And realize that being together
Is the highest state of my fulfillment

Last Love

A cry comes from the other room
And she rises from her dreams.

Sometimes the visions reveal her as
Pretty and wholesome, lively and fun-loving,
Within a circle of friends who admire
As much as adolescence will permit
While her radiance streams toward everyone.

Sometimes as a young woman, modestly
Seeking her mate, full of charm and grace,
Kindly and thoughtful, and naturally ready
To offer her affection to one
Who knows how to accept it.

Sometimes as a mother among her children
Warm with the joy of filling needs
For food and play and comfort after hurts,
Vaguely aware that the impulse to create
Is at work in their self-fashioning.

Sometimes in the fullness of her powers
Among the women of her worlds
Free to act out the inner sense
That an indifferent world will respond
To the efforts of sincere concern.

But she rises from these dreams
When the cry comes from the other room.
His need is now for a mother once again
As shapeless fear drives him toward escape
Into the imagined safety of his self.

She still retains the qualities
Of all her dreams, for they
Have formed her life and now
Make tolerable the residue
Of his existence.

And so at last the question is:
What is the final truth of love?
Love shows itself in many ways
At different times, but always from
The essence of our being,

And always as the work
Of the child within us
Who can teach us that
Love is, at last,
The destruction of the self.

Poems

for Thinkers

Holding On To Reality

Reality is like a beautiful rocky cliff
High, perpendicular, and at its base
A crashing, foamy sea.
We walk along a ledge
Half way up the cliff and
Far above the sea.
The ledge is wide
But there is no rail
Or other external support
To hold on to.
Most of us simply walk along
And pay no attention to the wonders of the cliff
Or to the dangers of the sea.
Some of us cower along the side of the cliff
And try to find or make
A fingerhold against the gusts
Of storms that come and go.
Some of us look at the cliff
And some at our feet
And some few fall over the edge
Into the sea.
The cliff remains unmoved.
It is the only thing that is.

The Critical Mass Establishes Itself

who knows

what's any good?

I say

well I'm not sure

and I say

why I don't know

and you say

why I'm not sure

and you say

well I don't know

and we say

they don't

that's sure

and we say

sometimes

you do

and we say

why yes

we do

By Thought, Word, and Deed

Rx: As Directed

Take mind deep thoughts

On rising in the morning

And scatter them abroad

As seed thanks for the day.

Take heart deep words

In gaps of understanding

And let them lead the way

Between the troubled sides.

Take soul deep deeds

In time of tribulation

And throw them all away

Beyond the reach of self.

When Things Go Wrong, The Fault Can Generally Be Pinned On The Other Fellow

I wonder why
you don't speak to me
you don't tell me
what you feel
why you don't
why you leave me keeping
a vigil of anticipation
that is about to blow me open
and extrude the parts
that I say are not in my machine
that I don't know how to handle
that are death to hide
like anxiety and fear
like anger and resentment
I wonder why

To a Beautiful Young Woman Who Keeps Being Attracted to Older Men

Dear, why do you keep on
Making the same mistake
Over and over again?
You don't need another father,
I'm sure of that--the one you have
Is plenty or maybe more than enough.
And men don't have to be old
To be reliable and considerate
If that's what you're after.
If you're looking for someone
To mother and take care of,
They come in all ages and styles and shapes
And the older ones tend to be
More troublesome in the long run,
And anyway it's better just to go ahead
And have babies of your own.
Or maybe you want to be the baby
And have someone take care of you:
I don't think that will work
For a spunky, intelligent person like you,

Full of a sense of independence
And clear about your own worth.
You'll always have to be explaining
Why the course of action proposed
Is illogical or undesirable,
And other people don't really enjoy
Having their lack of good sense exposed.
Have you been thinking about the possibility
Of just following the instincts of your heart
To see what happens?
Maybe so. Maybe that is best.
Then you can look for some satisfaction
In suffering the consequences,
Whatever they may be.

A Woman Meditating On Herself

I hardly ever meet any interesting men
Who aren't gay or securely married
Or unbelievably old. Everywhere, all around.
The people at work are either consumed
By the hope for success and concentrate
Whatever talents they have on trying to get ahead,
Or else they're hurting inside from their sense of inadequacy
And just want to lick their wounds
And stay alive and keep their jobs.
Oh, I make an effort to get around.
At those singles gatherings in Encino or Thousand Oaks
Or wherever, some of the people you meet
Are downright scary, and the others make me jumpy
In their eagerness to be impressive and feel good
About themselves by scoring with every woman they meet.
And have you ever read anything more disgusting
Than those personal ads in the paper under "Men Seeking
   Women",
In which it is clear that sincerity has disappeared
From the face and body of the earth
And has been replaced by the vain effort to be clever.

The men you meet through friends
Are mostly like merchandise that was returned for credit
Because of some serious defect, but the loyal friends
Hope there was some mistake in the earlier transaction
And you will be attracted to them and thus prove
That their friendship is soundly based.
Some men can be amusing for a little while
In one way or another, but there's not one among them
With whom I want to form a strong relationship.
My job is exciting and exhausting, and I use
My left-over energy in volunteer work and
Exercise classes and hiking on the week ends with Sierra
Club people
And lots of reading. My life is full to overflowing
And yet something seems to be lacking.
I could start law school in the evenings
Or take up Zen or get some psychiatric counseling.
I wish I had a friend.

An Invitation To Remember Or Forget

Somewhere within us, all of our experiences
Are said to be recorded
Permanently, forever.
The more we know about microcircuitry
And genetic structure and the controlling effect
Of a single particle in the DNA chain
The more plausible the thought can seem.
  I wonder about people I once knew
And haven't heard of since
And think I have, for all useful purposes, forgotten.
What about Newton Eubanks?
I think that we played together
But I don't recall a single detail
Nor even what he looked like--
All that I know about him is his name.
Or Hetty Sweeney, of whom I remember
Only that she was dark and plump
And that her father ran the Highland Park Hotel.
My memory of Laura Sledge
Is limited to the fact that we sometimes
Danced together at parties
Because my mother intimated that it was polite
To dance with all the girls and not just with

Rosa, Lida, Olivia, Dede, Percy, Mildred,
And other special friends.
I can remember Geissler Ashhurst a little better
Because he was a whiz at tennis and at telling fibs
And I can visualize his two older half-brothers
And his younger sister and his flighty mother
And yet I have the feeling that there must have been
More to him and to our relationship than that,
As I believe that we were once real friends.
So it goes. How about
Carlos Townsend and T. B. Hallman and
Grace Tarver and Lily Henderson and . . .
Oh, the names run on and on, and
There are doubtless many other people in the past
Even whose names have been entirely lost in my mind,
Along with all their human qualities.
  Are these people less real because I can't
Remember them at all or with anything like
The vividness which I am sure
That they possessed?
If so, forgetting would be an easy form
Of punishment to mete out.
("You had better treat me well,

Or else I will forget you and then
You will partially cease to exist.")
Which seems a godlike view of
The nature of reality.
   Or am I the one who is less real
Because I seem to have lost part of my self
When I have lost part of my past?
That's a human view, all right,
Because we have a deep fear of forgetting
And associate it with growing old
And losing our ability to keep
In reciprocal touch with the people of our world.
And yet we know that a perfect memory
Would burden us with an intolerable weight
Of the trivial and transient and irrelevant.
Is remembering a proof of reality, then,
Or only a clever mental trick
Practised in place of some more useful
Occupation of the mind?

The Influence Of Television On Growing Up

A Talk Show Symposium

Host. We are here today to discuss
The impact of television on us
As we grow up. May we
Share our experiences with one another,
And with all of you out there.
Let me ask you
What shows you saw
When you were growing up
And what they meant to you.
Mr. A, how about you?

Mr. A. Well, I grew up, so to speak, in the Fifties
And in our family we looked at TV
Only on Sunday afternoons
After Church and after our Sunday dinner.
The only shows I can remember
Are "Omnibus" and "Victory at Sea".

Host. And what are your recollections
Of those shows?

Mr. A. Well, I remember that the host
Of "Omnibus" was a man
Named Alistair Cooke.
He had a very serious but pleasant manner
And he had a funny way of speaking,
Kind of put on, foreign, though he was nice looking,
A little like my Uncle Joe,
Who moved away to the North.
"Victory at Sea" was full of action,
All kinds of ships going every whichway
Shooting at other ships
And at anything else in sight,
With lots of dark clouds
Overhead and on the horizon.
Everything moved fast
And seemed to be in a hurry.
The main thing about it was the music,
So strong and loud you had to cover your ears.
I guess it was planned for older people
Who didn't hear so well.

The episodes were sort of scary
But they all came out all right,
And we always won.

Host. Thank you. These are very helpful comments.
Now, Miss B,
What do you remember
About the TV shows
That you watched
When you were growing up?

Miss B. I grew up in the Sixties
And in our family we were
Allowed to look for an hour
If we had finished our homework,
And the three children had to take turns
Choosing what they wanted to see.
When it was my turn,
I chose "I Love Lucy"
Or "The Ed Sullivan Show"
Whenever I had the chance.
I liked them because
They made me feel better about myself.

Lucy was somewhere between silly
And addle-pated, and her husband
Wasn't around when they were
Passing out the brains.
Ed Sullivan mumbled out his introductions
As if he were trying to learn how
To recite the alphabet.
Of course I thought that some of his acts,
Like the Beatles, were terrific,
But most of all I thought
That if these dumb people
Could become prominent
Surely I would be able
At least to survive
In the adult world.

Host. Thank you, Miss B.
Those are very helpful comments,
And we are glad to have them
As your contribution to our inquiry.
And now, Mrs. C.,
What shows did you look at
When you were growing up?

Mrs. C. I grew up in the Seventies
And I looked at lots of TV
All the time. As I remember,
They were mostly comedy shows.
Some of them were pure farce,
Like "Mash" and Sid Caesar
And Imogen Coca. And some of them
Tried to give an amusing account
Of the way people supposedly lived, like
"All in the Family" or "Ozzie and Harriet".
Some people, like Mort Sahl,
Tried to make fun of everything.
I didn't actually think that any of it
Was very funny.
But I looked at it anyway
And thought it was mostly trash.

Host. Thank you so much, Mrs. C.,
For your recollections
Of the TV of the Seventies.
And now, finally, Mr. D.,
Please tell us how it was for you?

Mr. D. *Well, as I was growing up in the Eighties*
I was interested in music most of all.
There were a good many programs
That I valued, but you had to be
On the look out to catch them.
I especially enjoyed "Live from Lincoln Center"
With its variety of programs
And also the Boston Pops Orchestra
And the occasional concerts
From Wolftrap. They were all
Exciting to me. I loved the way
The conductors made big arcs
With their arms, and looked at the ceiling,
And smiled at the music they were creating.
And I enjoyed watching the faces
Of the performers, especially the oboists
As they pursed their lips, and the cymbal players
Who had to be so careful to crash
Their cymbals together at just the right instant.
Oh, it was very exciting, all of it,
And I wished that I could play an instrument
Or go to some live concerts somewhere.
But you know how it is,

I got so busy with my work
And my car and my friends
That I had to let my
Interest in music go.

Host. Thank you very much, Mr. D.
All of you have given us a very moving account
Of the TV you saw
As you were growing up.

And this brings our symposium to an end.
We have heard what TV meant
To people growing up in four decades,
And I am sure we all agree
That it has been a shaping influence
On all of our lives.

Thinking of Wallace Stevens

(On the occasion of the acquisition by the Huntington Library
of his books and papers from his daughter Holly)

Four Poems About His World In the Subtropical Garden

I.

The World as a Little Romancer

I touch your hand
And the light-hearted world stands still
a moment
In pleasure, perhaps,
Trying to show approval of my
Good fortune

You touch my arm
And the light-headed world stands still
a moment
In delight, perhaps,
Encouraging you to try it
Once again

II.

The World as Anticipation

Standing together
        Your arms curve around my neck
                with affectionate reserve

I am afraid to breathe
        For fear I will displace
                this magic moment

I know this is your act
        Of kindness to balance
                unsought love

And yet I take it
        As a welcome sign
                of friendship

Hoping that its form
        Will sometime become
                reality

III.

The World as Watchtower

I watch your face with admiration
It is a beautiful face, yes,
expressive, friendly, with open smiles

I watch your face with simple joy
In meetings, at a table, in a company which
dissolves into your shadow

What I see is poise, intensity, and strength
commitment to some goal I only partly
understand

Your face seems most at peace
when you are most engaged in business

I watch the edges of your face
longing for clues about your deeper thoughts

I find them, sometimes, in a flash
of private laughter, a sidelong glance, a
momentary recognition

And they are worth a life of watching

IV.

The World as a Bowl Full of Mixed Up Wishes

1) I have a strong wish
To write a poem for you
A poem about human relations
A poem that won't embarrass you
Even though it will have to be
Ultimately a poem about you
Since you are the center
Of my thoughts about human relations.

2) The wish is a hope to please
You more than myself
A wish to encourage the radiance that so often
Shines out from within you
A wish to avoid having to see
Those up and down lines in your lips
When your displeasure or uncertainty
Transmits signs of doubt.

3) Poetry is a form of discourse
With a rhetoric that we both
Think we understand
And so I can imagine having confidence
In myself for once to speak to you
In a common tongue about yourself
And wish that I could say it right
If only I knew what to say.

4) Lost in a world of words
That won't quite serve
And gestures that like slang
Offer too wide a range of choice
Lost in a world of evasion
To keep from coming to terms
With out of season feelings
That may or may not be absurd.

In Philosophical Hall

The American Philosophical Society
Held at Philadelphia
For Promoting Useful Knowledge

I

Our heroes watch over us
Observing what we try to do.
Benjamin Franklin there in the center,
Our founder, in the largest portrait,
Painted by Charles Willson Peale
And given to the Society by him
In 1783.
On the right George Washington
By Gilbert Stuart, 1797,
Bought from the artist in 1803.
On the left Thomas Jefferson
Drawn from the life by Thomas Sully
And here since 1821.
On our flanks stand two marble busts,
The Marquis de Condorcet on the left,
And on the right, Franklin yet once more.

II

Under their gaze
We sit in concentration, listening
To people of learning, philosophers,
Deliver their thoughts on today's developments
And what they can be made to mean
In the subjects they know best,
Their papers condensed to twenty minutes each
And put into language that we all
Think we can understand:
John Calvin's Anxiety, and
Plate Tectonics in Geoforms and Jigsaws, and
Ancient Maya Politics, and
Future Food Production, and
Nitrogen Metabolism in Coral-Algal Symbiosis, and
Businessmen and Business Culture in Imperial Russia, and
Biological Roots of Violence.
Something like that, rich intellectual fare
For the hungry human mind that has the love of knowing.
All day long, more, much more:
Some Thoughts Concerning the Importance of Pattern in
Diverse Systems, and

Medieval Cosmology, and
Nerve Growth Factor, and
Originality and Imitation in Modern Poetry, and
Genius and Milieu.
We come even from the edges of the earth
To focus our attention on these matters.

III

Our heroes have listened to
A lot of useful knowledge in their time.
In the earlier years they heard
Remarks on the Dental System of the Mastodon, and
Thoughts on the Influence of Ether on the Solar System, and
Observations upon the Meteors of August 1838, and
The Chinese System of Writing, and
The Decomposing Power of Water at High Temperatures, and
The Comparative Etymology of the Yoruba Language, and
On California Mosses.

IV

And how do our heroes respond
To all this pouring out of useful knowledge?
They are quietly listening with attention,
Absorbing and evaluating what we say,
Taking it all in
As part of the world's great body of knowledge,
As something more to deal with.
Franklin is also reading, but that's
Just like him, with so much to be accomplished
He has to do two things at once
And be a little skeptical about them both.
Washington maintains his dignity, tight-lipped,
Looking at the tops of our heads,
Giving us our chance and withholding judgment
Until we have finished,
Then he will be ready to respond.
Jefferson is gazing away from us
But pleased with what he hears
And (maybe more) by the visions and the dreams
That keep passing through his mind.
They seem to feel that there is

More they want to know:
Not to try to encompass all knowledge
But to enjoy this exercise of the intellect
And try out
New subjects and new ways
 Of dealing with them and
New ways
 Of thinking and
New ways
 Of play.
They encourage us to keep on considering
What other useful knowledge we can offer them.